Answer to My Ellipsis
-Donella M. Dornwell-

To Brian,
In gratitude
for your time!

Donella M.
Dornwell

Transcendent Zero Press

Houston, Texas

PUBLISHED BY TRANSCENDENT ZERO PRESS

Editor@transcendentzeropress.org

ISBN-13: 9781499756302

ISBN-10: 1499756305

Library of Congress Control Number: 2014942214
Printed in the United States of America

Transcendent Zero Press
www.transcendentzeropress.org

16429 El Camino Real Apt. 7
Houston, TX 77062

Cover Design: AJ Price Design

FIRST EDITION
Transcendent Zero Press

CONTENTS

To Mareena: May you always find hope in this world

"Hope" is the thing with feathers -
That perches in the soul -
And sings the tune without the words -
And never stops - at all −

--Emily Dickinson

Author's Note:

In the midst of illness, health, pain, sadness, and longing I wrote these poems as therapy. Many times I didn't think I would make it another day, but somehow I did. This book is my journey from the darkness of mental illness and back again. I believe along the way, hope has helped me through it all.

Donella as a Child

Young me being outside
eating cream, orange colored
honeysuckle juices while
playing cashier alone,
grass, twigs my groceries.

Barefoot but jaunting in
a sticker-filled lawn
catching small, green lizards.
Rubbing firefly guts on
my shirt at night making
me beam, glow-in-the-dark.

On tippy toes being
my own ballet–dreaming,
singing, twirling to my
own made up new tunes, then
older me sunbathing
in maroon bikini.

Me as a teenager
picking blackberries in
my backyard, loving my
unseen, lonely childhood...
No one in sight but me.

December 30, 2010

Liberty Lunch in Austin

1992 at Liberty Lunch
They Might Be Giants and Violent Femmes concerts,
stepping on broken beer bottles,
and feet crushed by Doc Martens.
Sweating in the front of a
General Admission crowd.

Mosh pits
and energetic masses
of young fans,
meshing with music,
melting pot of noise.

Reverberating in humidity,
air full of guitar fire
and youth, sweet youth.

I'm dancing back to
Liberty Lunch, 1992.

Twirling Prima Ballerina Donella

little me
Twirling
in the grass
'til my stomach ached

Twirling
on my tippy toes
on my life's
unstable stage

Twirling
to the music
in my head

Twirling
like a ballerina
on fire
laughing happily

Twirling
'til I felt drunk
dizzy in the head

Twirling
'til day turns
into nightmares

Twirling
in the center of
a roulette wheel

Twirling
into the kind
of woman
I am today.

April 27, 2010

Pushover

Let me introduce myself:

I'm self-deprecating,
amenable to others.
what he said was
"You're a pushover."
but really *I'm* evaporated,
saying "yes" to *them*
but "no" to me.

Shoving me out of happy
and into dim thoughts
of menial me
like lowly, weak,
and cowardly.

It's the door-matted closet
of dreads I've been.

I've submitted
to "any wind can
blow you."
They have my number.

So demean
me some more.
Those razors
of words don't hurt...
I mean, I've already
clipped my own wings...

But someday
I'm going to jump, crash,
bang into oblivion's
quiet resolution.
(and would that finally
make *them* happy?)

Radio Wars

We've made radio
     wars
of you and me...

those sultry night after night
    within Austin's borders.
When we "slept"
    radios blaring...

we fought with the knobs
    Turned–
        mine louder,
    Turned–
        yours loudest
back and forth our
    ears did tread.

Those battle lines were
    crossed between
My sedative, uneasy, melancholy
    tunes
and Your earthy, authentic, twangy
    ballads.

Our peaceful respect
    shot down
by ever-increasing
    Volumes,
With no diplomacy
    In all that noise...

we never even Heard
    each other's favorite
        Song.
Yet those solemn
    casualties
aren't quite carried away
    in the past's musically
        chaffing, barren wind.

~For Mimmi

November 19, 2010

College Dress

What she said was:
"You're college material."

I'm not that much (of course).
I'm some twill,
cotton-blend, silk
textile-type,
yet with all that
material
I'll make a
simple muslin dress.

I made a collage,
a new seam in me,
sew me some more.

In all that
excess fabric,
this patchwork
of a quilted
life with no
"college" in it.

Come a little closer &
strip a pretty
dress out of
a shop window...

that's how I make it.

Answer to My Ellipsis

before...during...after...

that illness.

there has finally been
that long-standing answer
to those lone three
after an extended

Period.period.period.

preceded by the "help me!" prayer
desperate for health,
a reprieve,
the inevitable
Continuation.

always wondering
what next is
to follow...
        I pray to the Lord...
                Lord, hear my prayer.

Bridges Like Rumi's

Bridge to eternity
friends of all creation:
plant, animal, mineral,
human, water, food.
Breaking the bread
bridges the gaps
of disbelief with belief
finding friends in
unlikely places
where prayer seems
infinitely intangible.

Certifiable

My credibility is askew now
that I'm certifiable.

Even though the medicine
spins away that certificate

like a leaf on the way down a creek.

It is my diploma I've earned
through life's varied battles.

In that classroom I learned of
self-hatred, greed, and partiality.

When I was earning the next degree
of separation from the high school,

I found that love did exist
in the form of a motherly bond.

But the certificate had to be sealed
with the official notification

to the world that, yes, I did deserve that title;
For I earned it in just two weeks

it simply required a hospital stay.
But no pain killers were allowed.

Only a bed with whole white sheets
to rest my head and dream

of the freedom that escapes me even now.
For once you've earned the degree

the only thing is to
live up to it.

And once I find that wandering leaf
that seemed to wash away,

hopefully I'll find more love
in some other creek.

Carved to Pieces for You

Every day a
piece of me
is chipped away,

chiseled off
that wood so carved.
Bit by bit,
every sawdust speck,
particle, and atom
dissipates a little
more each day.

There are microscopic bites
some mild days,
glacial chunks break off
those panicking days,

but every day
a piece of me
is taken
and sent in
envelopes of various
sizes and mailed
to You whose
so far away

Over seas and seas
away from me.

May 1, 2010

Be a Good Girl and Make Your Bed

Like that
unmade bed
unmake this mind
psychotropic drugs
unmade that
awkward unbalance.
Un-take those pills
and where would you be?

Back in the
hospital hell.
Kiss those covers,
sheets to bare skin,
refreshingly cool.
Does that mean the
hollow heat in you
can now escape?

Full of pillows
propping you up
and rose-covered
pill cases
hiding the
severity of need for
those corrective
empty crevices
concealing your brain's
Fitted sheet–
cured of primary, saturated
Color.

Disease

The goal: the tight rope
walk of stable me...

this fragile nature
of me, up to the
stars, light years and years
from sane, from safe, then
down to the ocean
floor...miles and miles
to descend...the battle

of the moods...fight back!

These duplicitous
emotions dually
dwelling in this state.

It's the difference
between peace and war,
the same love and hate,
so much light and dark...

My final defeat:
the obsession I
feel the need to feed...

"Please, just let me breathe!"

October 22, 2007

donella sense

my brother would say
I lack the common of it all

for how could I still cling
to the thought of you

but common is for the
birds I sense

since I left you
I've none left

rationalize what you will
I am irrational still

but who could make
judgement on this fervent desire

I've come to the conclusion
that it's simply donella sense.

April 3, 2009

I have a little bit of Crazy in me!

Just a tidbit

Something teeny-weeny

It creeps up in a hurry

Nothing too serious (this time)

It's masked in paranoia

That only I can perceive

Little iota

A little some-some

Come and get me

It can't be undone

You say I'm quirky

I say love-love

It's senseless, I know

Itty bitty little baby bits of it

Eating away my insides...

Just a bit!

January 21, 2012

Eyes

I'm caught by Your
orbs: mahogany painted pearls
their gaze enveloping me.

Give me a tawny
glimpse: a glint of
Your Soul.

March 4, 2012

I Do Things for a Reason *(Las Preguntas)*

Why did I leave?

...because it hurt to breathe when I was separated from you and I would have suffocated if you had deserted me instead.

...because my sleep was so interrupted I saw visions of you in every place I visited, in every book I perused.

...because food was no longer necessary and my body was in revolt...it needed sustenance.

...because just the sight of you made me sad that I'd never touched you and probably never would.

...because I was afraid that I'd finally know what love was if I let you in and that terrified me then and still does now.

Why can't I forget you?

...because maybe I saw a glimpse of love then and maybe I never will again.

In Memory of 2000, When We Met

Silver essence memories,

crushing my serenity.

your solemn, seeking...serious eyes,

thumbtacking thoughts of you and

those orbs right where you

sought mine.

Loss:

the oceans's last wave

still yet longing...

the sea's breath is depleted,

the shell's forgotten her sparkle and glint,

the wind's caught and swept under a skirt...

the moon sacrificed to zero gravity...drifting away.

But maybe,

someday our hands might

touch, when gravity resumes, like...

Moon ships land.

Christmas Presence

I'm letting the past pummel me,
those past Christmases,
with and without you,
escape from red-ribbon and
black fringe benefit heels:
a present for the remember.

an entry into the chasm
of my cobwebbed mind
dusty with the lack of
your sentiments...judge me,
how the perfection of the feelings
contrast the utter imperfection of me.
a continual red light, foot glued
to the brake—immobile once more.
going through the motions of these
emotions—(and the alternative?)

letting you slip through
my culpable hands as I stir
from sleep again and again.

Kept Clothes

Granny's vintage dress
Elena altered into
Mini sexy teenage cool.

Mexican floral dresses
once danced...
flattened between
cloth piles of trash.

holey snowflake pajamas
mommy & me
both wore
don't mind being
hers after all.

man's armor:
black and white flannel,
last ties to sweet father,
worn torn in mania–

these are closeted
strings played
between family,
cloaked genes just
won't let up.

April 3, 2009

Love Bites

I want a bit of a bite of you

Just a little slice

Ok, I'll settle for a sliver

Yeah, that makes me quiver

Don't deny me the sensation

Of knowing how you feel

For just the touch of you

Brings me to the brink

How can you be so stoic?

It's the masculine in you...I see it

You just don't know it,

But I see right through you.

Yeah, I'm a good read a little late at night

But you are the bite of it

That only I can chew

Knowing I was meant for you.

June 17, 2013

Lovely One

Lovely one,
I engulf your body
with my able arms,
strong open wide

For you.

Lovely one,
your eyes have surrendered,
unabashed as they
take me in for

A taste.

Lovely one,
lips cascade, languid kisses,
yours dewy, sweet
they encompass

Us tonight.

Lovely one,
your voice is symphonic,
the bluesy wonders
rolling of your tongue
savings their suppressions for

Another day.

June 7, 2010

My Kind of Mania

It begins with
ominous sleeplessness
that builds my energy
until the frothing fuzziness
consumes me–eating away
like battery acid, all
my chemical-induced happiness.

Then edgy, anxiety
is morphed into
a blurring silvery-gray aura
surrounding me.

Appetite is depleted,
my nauseated, stale,
heavy stomach.

It's a hyper-attentive state,
every self-conscious thought
full of meaningful
paranoid essence and those
hidden cameras at every corner!

Those thoughts expressing
EVERYTHING in one
pregnant moment that
exudes action with
every wicked turn
of my mind's page,
turning pages into the
jumble of constant conspiracy.
(But how could it be?)

Fog filling in the
empty spaces,
replacing rationality
with grandiose religious ideation.

Skipping logical reality
in exchange for the
Height of the World's attention
--That high!

Can't escape
fidgety pacing
up and down stairwells
of confusing delusion.

The rampant rushing
thoughts become
an uneasy, shaky
scene of a never-ending
cliff of emotions.

Memory is now
altered eternally
into blacked out
phases until I'm
grasping for futile recollection.

Then I am most vigorously
Erased-
it's that twisted
tangle of a proxy person
I've been.

On the Nights I Saw You

A cold glazed look crosses my face
as I think of you then
              and again and then and again...

You saw just the tip,
but this me–is an iceberg
               looming
under the surface;
far too much to be seen.

And how much did I see?
           Did I see a piece of you?
                          Will I yet?

I'll keep you hidden like the
stars and moon in my back (night) pocket
              -just for me.

Pasta Pieces

When you're
falling apart
there's no one
there to catch
the pieces you
turn into
like pieces of pasta
caught in a colander.

You just come apart
and sink down the drain
like boiling water...
boiled in your own skin.

January 10, 2009

Puer et Puella

You are the *puer*
Me the *puella*

We met during the darkest of nights, etc.
My life was at its lowest low

You were my highest high
This was not just puerility

Maybe I spoke Latin
and you English

Perhaps we played
a puerile game

But to me, the "good girl"
You were the "good guy"

No childishness could compare
No game amongst adults could lead
to the *mulier et vir* we have become today

Vale, my love.

December 10, 2011

Weight of a Minute

Minutes:
pile up on me,
make their mark,
dandelion days,
yellowing years

life's hiking trail
of magnificent but
miniscule matters:

running towards
what's tantamount to a
tangling tunnel of time,
fostering forever.

but always wondering:
how many more do I have left?

My Consuming Song

My consumption of
that long used up love
has been sustenance,
the very marrow
of the matter now.
It's been rich, deeper
than his dark lake eyes,
this mind food of mine.

Now I'm floating low,
replacing that love
with this starvation,
a birdseed deprived
mockingbird aper
singing these varied,
harried, salient songs.

The Sense of Water

How can my senses

Make water more alive?

Its trickle, drip, and sync with me

Soaking my throat with its salve

Music in the melodic movement,

Cascading towers that fall

To a pool at my feet

Then I dangle my toes inside it

With a slow strum of its shadow on me

Clean, fresh, instantaneously.

Tears

Dry me up!
These desert mirages, the regrets.
Don't choke back this rain.

Sprinkling, drizzling...
life's condensation.
These aren't just any
eye precipitations...
like mine,
completely arbitrary (of course!)

Showering, flooding...
streaking down my cheeks,
the window-pains of my soul.

I need tons of
tissue umbrellas
for this tanker full of
tears.

Sir Lancelot in the Mix

Pills: my knight
in capsule clothing,
downing prescription narcotics–
addicted, used, confused, come undone.

Can't demolish this
barricade I've accumulated:
too high to conquer.
                 and even with this disease–
still too strong to concede defeat.

I'd like a new knight,
The kind I took with
my last break/relapse.

I'm a bit better.
This combination of drugs
and brain chemicals
mesh my life
Into peanut butter mush

I'm mixed-up with
no reprieve.

September 23, 2012

Radioactive Recovery

Radioactive hysteria!
Then a concoction of meds:
atomic bomb for the mind,
mushroom cloud in my brain
contaminated ground water
synapses firing blanks–

Bi-polar recovery style:
I've lost my carcinogenic thoughts,
skull and cross bones on this
bottled up poison person
whose withstood the propensity
to regress into malformed mania,
at least for awhile...

Pharmaceuticals in hand,
succumbed to mealy emotions,
unrecognizable, numb, stabilized.

March 29, 2010

Six Months of Night

Captured night,
made it my own.
Though starless and void,
I called it home.

Found You in
that time so bleak...
waxing and waning
into this
　　　　new moon in me.

But in those lunar months,
the day did break
the dark tethers
I'd created.

Now You remain
that dawning morning's
placid and beaming
　　　　Peak.

October 13, 2010

Not Just Any Ex-Homo Sapien

I'm only a monster shell
I'm another species now
that I'm transformed into
this, it's not self-deprecating
I can't reconcile that once
sane me with this new creature:
medicated, but still far away...

I'm fragile, not so scary
weak and prone to sleeplessness
and depression and panic

The older me is ruined
replaced with longing, longing.

I'm tainted, paranoia
caught me, made me this sick me.

I'm driven to delusion,
dark, deceptive, damaging
but still the longing, longing.

This she-monster resides in
me, this foreign species me
every step I take is a
step void of stability.

I'm left with so much of this
pitiful longing, longing.

Snowflakes

shine on you this
radiant morning;
awaken to a view
of frosted trees and
pristine flurries kissing your face
containing the Lord's divine order,

there's no simple clear pattern,
they make up intricate
earthy constellations,
these stencils of mirth
not obscured like clouds,
they are denotations of Christ's peace:

transcending the bleakest of nights,
remembering the promise of spring.

To: S.W., the disillusioned 2

When I fell into the abyss of my own mind
It was a swirling, whirling undertow that allowed me to come up for breathes every
so often only to pull me back under with tackling tugs and I could do nothing...

I simply sank and allowed myself to fall deeper into that drowning dank water
Those cerebral fluids, those damned chemicals directing my thoughts.
What a wicked imbalance!

I tried though how I tried to grasp at something to keep me afloat.
The driftwood was fleeting and few and far between.
But when I did manage to cling one of those pieces of timber, you were that piece.

And how can I blame you for letting me drown?
You didn't know how to swim in those murky waters yourself.
You didn't grow up with those types of diagnoses.

You simply floated on by and snubbed me.
I thought you would be my life preserver and yet you were unwilling.
You weren't trained in a psyche ward for life guards after all.

You Feed Me

I am a
lecherous leech
feeding off you
frantic...
piranha jaws,
eating you to the
ordinary bone.

Puncturing kisses,
as I detach–
no sweet blood
only bitter elixir.
That I spit
–it's acid.
This efficacy
makes me puke.

These are putrid
red hot happenings.

May 2012

Abrir

I devour a piece of mind's pie,
bite it like the enchilada dinner,
a present from my unmedicated sister

in the mental hospital in January.

Remembrances of the dying
Laguna Gloria garden,
how beautiful spring might be
mixed with the sugar
of a visit from my four year old,

a piece I open up for every day since...

Like when the skies opened and sent me
that delusional haze–in the midst, a face,
her light shining in a bleak winter rain.

I eat up that pie like I wanted to eat
the storybook *Beauty and the Beast*
I'd savor pieces of over and over because it's
saturated with love, the kind I've never tasted,
but I became this beast instead.

Eating poisoned food
in a sectioned tray in the
hospital dining hall
while seeing my piece of mind
and that peace of pie,

I close my mouth and chew it
again and again,
hoping it will taste right this time.

June 23, 2008

Cascades

Like a waterfall
the mental illness
cascades over any
possibility of the "happy ending"

But I still long for it.

I want you to cascade
this chemical imbalance
like you did once before

you transcend
the torment of losing
my mind

you are the waterfall
I could hide behind

You are that pure
drink of water
that washed away

all the pain.

January 18, 2010

Again & Again

each day it happens...
I implode
with cancerous emotion
    Again & again...

It causes the Bends
as I scuba up
for air.

What carcinogens
I breathe
eating up my lungs
as I sob
for You
    Again & again...

April 15, 2014

Egging to Get Over Depression

Take a look into my mind
Life shrinking into a tiny ball,
Depression, full breath pressure:
No sound because music dwindles.
No love because passion falters then
A cracked egg of a shell,
The yolk of myself
Feeding off of
Listless, frustrated hunger,
An egg white tasteless little life
Wanting to break into so much more.

Decisions

I am more than what meets my life.
Decisions like tongue suppressors,
melting in my salivating mouth,
nodding at each fickle, flagrant
suggestion.

Turning from stomach aching dependence,
flocking like sparrows,
filling the skies with new types,
soaring to bring me closer to this:
signing away this crooked life.

Mind over spongy thought saturation,
those semi-pressed lies of agreement.
I'm going to choose this time.

Mellowed

I'm softer: not so cognizant hard,
more moderate and mellow
tension mollified and melted
pliant pieces of puzzle me

shaped into elasticity in my seams
that rubber sling holding me
subdued but not depleted
relenting, slack, surreal

assuaging the anxiety,
unwound and fluffed
marinated in ease
bathing in warm not scalding water

beginning to boil under not over
basking in baby better
loose and limber likened to lax laughter
sighing with simplicity

intensity shredded into snow-like
feathering flow of confetti calm.

Silence

silence, the sequester
the jury, my judge
the confinement, my punishment
selfish and damaged
given that piece of the pie,
the slice that was forgotten
on a full stomach:
wasted away that piece
like a life that lost its luster.
Wake-up to a new sunshine tomorrow.

Pigeon

Homing pigeon
carries that remedy
rolled in each note
sent back and forth
from nowhere to
your mind's home
that is full of blue skies
that antidotal perch.

Recuperating
from those
capsules of losses
and regaining a sense
of life's nest:
an endless Wonder.

ACKNOWLEDGEMENTS

Thank you to my family and friends who have supported me during my life's journey. This book took years to write and I was inspired by all of you along the way. Special thanks to Angela Jackson who helped me decide on which poems should come first and which should come last. Thank you to AJ and Dustin at Transcendent Zero Press for realizing my vision for my poems. To my late parents, William A. and Ardella M. Dornwell, thanks for all the unconditional love you gave me and my late grandmother, Mimmi, who raised me to believe in God. Many thanks to Mareena, my Hope above all hopes. Above all, I thank God for guidance, strength, and serenity for which He's granted time and time again.

About the Author...

Donella M. Dornwell has been writing poetry since she was thirteen. She had many poems published in literary magazines in middle school and high school. More recently she had poems published in the Austin International Poetry Festival's *di-verse-city* anthologies. She lives in Southern California near her daughter.

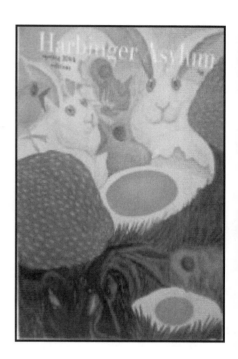

Look online at *www.transcendentzeropress.org*
for other fabulous collections of poetry!

From One Sphere to Another: Best of Harbinger Asylum 2010-12
(left)

Harbinger Asylum Spring 2014 edition
(right)

These and other fabulous titles are on sale at
Amazon.com.

Made in the USA
Middletown, DE
15 October 2022